Bitcoin: Technical Background and Data Analysis

Anton Badev   Matthew Chen[*]

October 7, 2014

Executive summary

Broadly speaking, Bitcoin is a scheme designed to facilitate the transfer of value between parties. Unlike traditional payment systems, which transfer funds denominated in sovereign currencies, Bitcoin has its own metric for value called bitcoin (with lowercase letter "b", and abbreviated as BTC[1]). Bitcoin is a complex scheme, and its implementation involves a combination of cryptography, distributed algorithms, and incentive driven behaviour. Moreover, recent developments suggest that Bitcoin operations may involve risks whose nature and proportion are little, if at all, understood. In light of these considerations, the purpose of this paper is to provide the necessary technical background to understand basic Bitcoin operations and document a set of empirical regularities related to Bitcoin usage.

We present the micro-structure of the Bitcoin transaction process and highlight the use of cryptography for the purposes of transaction security and distributed maintenance of a ledger. Our empirical analysis is based on publicly available transaction-level data. We examine patterns of general usage together with usage by Satoshi Dice, the largest online gambling service using Bitcoin as the method of payment. Our analysis suggests that less than 50 percent of all bitcoins in circulation are used in transactions. About

[*]Authors' affiliation: Federal Reserve Board, 20th and C Streets NW, Mail Stop 188, Washington, D.C. 20551. Corresponding author: Anton Badev (anton.i.badev@frb.gov). Disclaimer: The analysis and conclusions set forth are those of the authors and do not indicate concurrence by other members of the research staff or the Board of Governors. The authors would like to thank Francesca Carapella, May Liu, Mark Manuszak, Jeffrey Marquardt and David Mills for helpful comments.

[1]Others have used XBT to abbreviate bitcoin. In this paper we use BTC throughout as suggested in https://en.bitcoin.it.

half of these transactions involve less than U.S.$100 equivalent, and for the period for which we have data for Satoshi Dice, most of these small-value transactions were related to the online gambling service. Relatively less frequent large value transactions drive the average transaction value to levels above U.S.$40,000 equivalent value, and are not likely to involve payments for goods and services.

Bitcoin exchange rates exhibit somewhat complicated dynamics. In the past 24 months, the USD-BTC exchange rate increased more than 50-fold. Unnoticed by the public, however, the daily variance of the USD-BTC exchange rate remained remarkably stable for this same period, once the variance calculations account for the changing exchange rate level.[2] We also document that the exchange rates between bitcoin and other major currencies are not well aligned. We interpret this as lack of depth of the exchange markets and as costly exchange rather than as unexploited arbitrage opportunities. Finally, the appendix provides more details on updating the ledger, including a quantitative examination of the economic incentives for the participants in the distributed implementation of the Bitcoin system.

1 Introduction

The period after February 2013 witnessed developments of unprecedented scale for Bitcoin—a scheme that facilitates the transfer of value between parties and that, unlike traditional payment systems, has its own metric for value (called bitcoin, with lowercase letter "b", and abbreviated as BTC[3]). As of October 7, 2014 more than 64,000 businesses were reported to accept payments in bitcoins around the world, and the exchange rate was more than U.S.$300 to the bitcoin, which is more than 50 times higher than 24 months earlier.[4] In contrast to these positive developments, Mt. Gox, the largest bitcoin exchange, filed for bankruptcy in February 2014 after the announcement of a mysterious disappearance of bitcoins valued at almost U.S.$500 million.[5] These developments suggest that the apparent lucrative opportunities which Bitcoin presents may be surrounded by risks whose

---

[2]This finding, however, should not be interpreted as a prediction about forward-looking risk in holding bitcoins. See also footnote 9.

[3]Others have used XBT to abbreviate bitcoin. In this paper we use BTC throughout as suggested in https://en.bitcoin.it.

[4]With the exception for the number of businesses accepting bitcoin, these numbers are obtained from the data we discuss in section 4. The number of businesses accepting bitcoin is reported in (CoinDesk, 2014, The state of Bitcoin Q2 2014). However, we do not have information of how this estimate is obtained nor how accurate it may be.

[5]For more details on the incident see https://en.bitcoin.it/wiki/MtGox.

nature and proportion are little, if at all, understood.

Bitcoin, like cryptocurrencies generally, is a complex scheme. Its implementation involves a combination of cryptography, distributed algorithms and incentive driven behaviour. Moreover, these are recent phenomena and there is thin academic literature, a nascent policy debate, and limited understanding from the public about cryptocurrencies overall.

The purpose of this paper is to provide the necessary technical background for understanding Bitcoin's basic operations and to document a set of empirical regularities related to Bitcoin usage. It is important to emphasize that the goal of our empirical analysis is to be informative yet not dogmatic. In particular, we provide a series of observations with the aim of motivating substantive research, not of providing definitive assertions on the future of Bitcoin. Similarly, although we hope to inform the policy debate, our analysis does not focus on the legal, regulatory, and policy implications of Bitcoin.[6]

In the first part of the paper we discuss the micro-structure of the Bitcoin transaction process. The discussion pays special attention to the use of cryptography in the Bitcoin protocol. Specifically, the protocol uses cryptographic algorithms for the security of transactions and for the implementation of distributed maintenance of a public ledger. Our interest in cryptographic algorithms is also motivated by their use to enable distributed recordkeeping which has been noted to have potential applications, independently of the success of Bitcoin, to a broader set of economic practices reaching beyond the payment industry.

The second part of the paper presents an empirical analysis of transaction-level data which are publicly available from the Bitcoin system. The starting point of our analysis is identifying general patterns of usage. While we cannot tightly estimate the number of daily users, we note that it is likely to have grown exponentially. Our estimates suggest that the number of daily users has doubled every eight months.[7] Despite this growth, the daily transaction volume is still negligible compared to the domestic volume of U.S.

---

[6]For example, our discussion of the anonymity of Bitcoin relates to, but is not focused on, the use of Bitcoin to finance illicit activities. Similarly, while we provide background and document patterns of usage we do not explicitly assess the potential of Bitcoin to impact the US payment or banking system, or the conduct of monetary policy. Related discussions can be found elsewhere, including in GAO (2014), ICBA (2014), and EBA (2014).

[7]The available data have limited power not only for the estimation of the daily use but also for the estimation of the adoption speed. With respect to the latter we only point out that bitcoin adoption is subject to network externalities. Thus, everything else equal, it can take longer for schemes like Bitcoin to mature, i.e. to attract a critical mass of users. For more on network externalities in payments see Prager, Manuszak, Kiser and Borzekowski (2009).

payment systems, and even more so as compared to the overall volume of international payments. Looking at the composition of transactions, we note that about half of the transactions involves more than U.S.$100 equivalent value and drive the average transaction value to U.S.$40,000 equivalent value. For the period for which we have data for Satoshi Dice, most of the transactions involving less than U.S.$100 equivalent value can be attributed to the online gambling service.[8] These observations all together suggest that Bitcoin is still barely used for payments for goods and services.

The empirical analysis concludes with a set of observations which are broadly related to the use of Bitcoin for investment and payment purposes. In particular, we discuss the speed of recycling of bitcoin addresses and the nature of risk associated with holding bitcoins. More than half of the bitcoins in circulation have not been used in transactions the past three months and about a third have not been used in the past year. These overall statistics constitute an estimate of the proportion of bitcoins in circulation which are held for "investment" purposes. Next, we examine the dynamics of the bitcoin exchange rate. We argue that the vigorous growth in bitcoin value in the past 18–24 months has been accompanied by almost unchanged daily variance of the exchange rate once the variance calculations account for the changing exchange rate level.[9] This point has remained largely unnoticed because it cannot be readily inferred by the raw exchange-rate trends (typically reported by the media). Finally, the exchange rates between bitcoin and other major currencies are not well aligned. We interpret this as lack of depth of the exchange markets and costly exchange rather than as unexploited arbitrage opportunities.

The appendix contains additional materials related to the Bitcoin scheme, including more technical details on updating the ledger. The appendix also includes a quantitative examination of the incentives for participation in the distributed implementation of the Bitcoin system. Our analysis of past developments in the magnitude and the structure of the rewards lends support to recent concerns regarding the cost efficiency and the sustainability of the Bitcoin scheme (see Levine, 2014).

---

[8]Satoshi Dice is the largest online gambling service using Bitcoin as the method of payment. For the majority of its life, Satoshi Dice accounted for more than 40 percent of the overall bitcoin transaction volume. For more see section 5.3 on page 18.

[9]While we do not do this here, this observation merits further analysis. For example, such stable exchange rate variance could in principle be the result of activities by parties interested in the stability and trustworthiness of the system.

2 Bitcoin: an overview

The Bitcoin scheme carries attributes of a payment system in that it facilitates the transfer of value between parties. Unlike traditional payment systems, which typically involve the transfer of value denominated in a sovereign currency such as the US dollar, Bitcoin has its own metric for value called a bitcoin.[10] In essence, a bitcoin is an electronic token without reference to any underlying commodity or sovereign currency, and is not a liability on any balance sheet. Owning bitcoins amounts to nothing more than having the ability to move these bitcoins in the Bitcoin ecosystem (see section 3.2.1). As such, a bitcoin has no intrinsic value. Rather, a bitcoin's value is derived mainly from its use for making payments in the Bitcoin system, and from the purpose of accruing gains from bitcoins' possible appreciation. To our knowledge, a bitcoin has no legal tender status in any jurisdiction at the time of this writing.[11] Moreover, some economists have questioned whether bitcoins meet the standard attributes of money (see the discussion in Yermack, 2013, and Lo and Wang, 2014).

Figure 1 shows a diagram of payments on the Bitcoin users' network. The nodes are entities and the directed arrows depict payments in bitcoin. As the diagram suggests, the entities transact *directly*, that is, in contrast to most traditional payment systems where various parties, such as banks, processors, and networks, sit between the payor and payee, there is no designated intermediary in Bitcoin.[12] Each transaction is chronologically recorded in a *public* ledger, called the blockchain, by participants in the network. There is a reward for recording transactions in the blockchain, and the participants in the Bitcoin system compete (by solving a computationally intensive cryptographic problem) to make records. A well-defined process, which guarantees consensus, elects the winning participant and the blockchain is updated. Importantly, each participant keeps a copy of the ledger, and the consensus of the incremental changes guarantees that these copies are identical.[13] Thus, the verification and the record keeping of transactions is decentralized.

---

[10]We follow the convention of distinguishing bitcoin (with lowercase letter "b") from Bitcoin—the payment system. To our knowledge this distinction is used for no other virtual currency scheme.

[11]For a related discussion on the topic of consumers' risks, including the lack of customers' legal protection, see (ICBA, 2014, Virtual Currency: Risk and Regulation) and (EBA, 2014, Opinion on Virtual Currencies).

[12]Many businesses have recently emerged that make using Bitcoin more accessible. Thus, in practice, some of these businesses act as intermediaries. Unfortunately, our data does not allow us to estimate what percentage of the Bitcoin users transact directly as opposed through some type of service provider. For a related conceptual discussion see Lo and Wang (2014).

[13]The appendix (page 29) contains a closer discussion of the Bitcoin protocol. To avoid confusion, we only mention that the process of determining the main version of a blockchain ensures that it is the one created by a majority of the computational resources on the network.

Figure 1: The Bitcoin concept

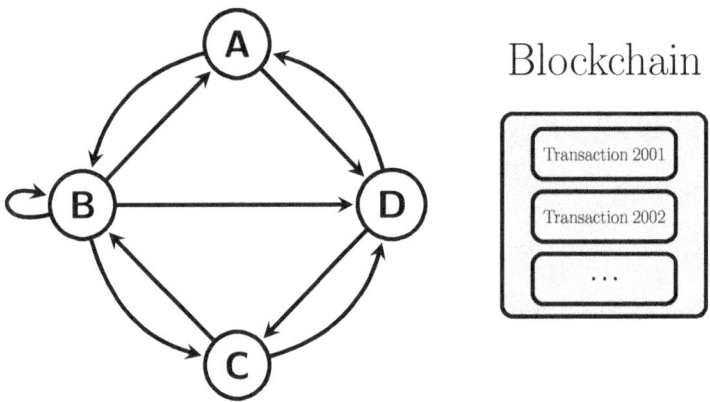

Note: *There are four entities A, B, C and D, transacting directly with each other, i.e. with no intermediary. In addition, the diagram shows the possibility of B transacting with itself. All transactions are chronologically recorded in a public ledger called a blockchain.*

The procedure for rewarding those who make records on the blockchain embeds the economic incentives driving the system and appears to "hard-code" the growth of the bitcoin supply. Specifically, the reward for recording a transaction includes a (voluntary) fee and newly minted bitcoins.[14] In fact, the latter is where the novelty of the Bitcoin scheme for governing the amount of bitcoins in circulation lies. Because the rate of making transaction records is stable over time, there is some certainty about the rate of growth of bitcoins (hence the amount of bitcoins in circulation, shown in figure 30 in the appendix). Moreover, because the rate of growth of bitcoins is set to decrease exponentially, the total amount of bitcoins is bounded at 21 million and the bound is expected to be reached in 2140.[15][16]

The Bitcoin transaction process is fairly complex and computer scientists are actively investigating aspects of its security, privacy, distributed control and incentive schemes. For example, although Bitcoin is referred to as a near-instantaneous payment system (on average it takes 10 minutes to process a transaction), some have questioned its suitabil-

---

[14]Recently, the magnitude and the structure of miners' rewards have attracted much public attention. In particular, concerns have been raised on the cost-efficiency of the system and on whether the incentives to maintain the distributed record-keeping are sustainable. Appendix B.2 (on page 31) provides a quantitative examination of miners' incentives and suggests further references.

[15]To be precise, the rate of recording transaction blocks (not individual transactions) is stable over time and the amount of newly minted bitcoins is specified per block of transactions.

[16]See https://bitcoin.org/en/faq.

ity for fast payments.[17] Further discussion of these topics is beyond the scope of this work; however, section 3 provides a technical yet accessible presentation of the bitcoin transaction process.

3 The Bitcoin transaction process

We now turn to describe the Bitcoin transaction process. Because cryptographic algorithms have implications for the security and privacy of Bitcoin's implementation, we start with a brief overview. Then we turn to describe a transaction record on the public ledger. Because the public ledger is the main source of information for the activity in the Bitcoin system, its structure naturally determines the scope of our empirical analysis. Finally, we present the process of executing a payment between two parties using the Bitcoin network.

3.1 Cryptographic basics

The Bitcoin transaction process uses cryptography to verify transactions, process payments, and control the supply of bitcoins.[18] The particular cryptographic schemes implemented in the Bitcoin protocol are not new and, in fact, are used in a wide range of information security applications. Because the topic is somewhat esoteric in economic applications and, more importantly, because we believe that cryptographic and distributed algorithms may have applications to a broader set of economic practices reaching beyond the payment industry, we review at some length the principles of their operation below.

Bitcoin relies on two cryptographic schemes: *digital signatures* and *cryptographic hash functions*. Briefly, the former enables the exchange of accurate (payment) instructions between the parties of a transaction, and the latter is used to enforce discipline in writing transaction records in the public ledger. Neither of these schemes is unique to Bitcoin; they are widely used to secure commercial and government communications. For the sake of completeness, we provide a brief outline below.

---

[17]Karame et al. (2012) argue that bitcoins can be double-spent in the context of fast payments. In fast payments the time between the payment and the delivery of goods or services is on the order of seconds, e.g. online services, ATM withdrawals, vending machine payments, etc.

[18]For this reason Bitcoin is often referred to as a **cryptocurrency**.

Figure 2: Public Key Encryption

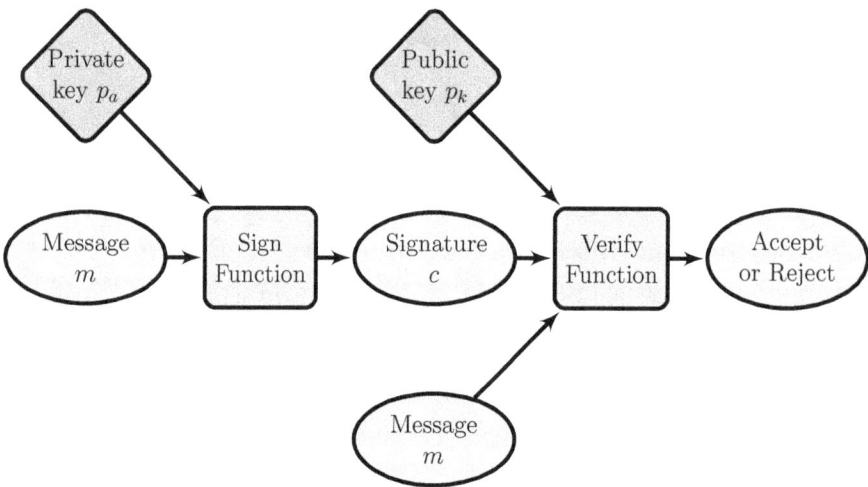

3.1.1 Digital signatures

Digital signatures are a way to authenticate a message between a sender and a receiver in a way that ensures:

(i) *authentication*: the recipient can verify that the message came from the sender,

(ii) *non-repudiation*: the sender cannot deny sending the message,

(iii) *integrity*: the message has not been tampered with.

The implementation of digital signatures involves *public key encryption*, where a pair of keys—public and private—are generated with certain desirable properties.

Figure 2 illustrates the process of digitally signing a message (or a unit of data). The "sign" function combines the message with the private key of the sender to produce signature c. The process of obtaining c is in effect signing the message with the identity of the sender, her private key p_a. The intended recipient then receives the signed message (the message m together with its signature c). Before accepting the message, the receiver verifies the authenticity of its sender by comparing the message and the public key of the sender. This is done by the "verify" function that takes as inputs the signed message (m and c) together with the public key p_k and produces a binary output state: accept or reject. The sign and verify functions are publicly accessible.

The Bitcoin protocol employs the above scheme to sign transaction messages. In particular, transaction m is signed with the private key p_a and then broadcast to the bitcoin network. All members of the Bitcoin system can verify that this transaction came from the owner of public key p_k by taking the message m, signature c, and public key p_k and running the verification algorithm.[19]

3.1.2 Cryptographic hash functions

In general, a cryptographic hash function takes as input a string of arbitrary length and returns a string with predetermined length. We will refer to the input as message m and the output as hash h. The function is deterministic, meaning that the same input m will always give the same output h. However, knowing the hash of the message reveals little if anything about the message. This is fundamental for hash functions and is more formally stated below.

1. *Pre-image resistance.* Given a hash h it is difficult to find a message m such that $\mathrm{hash}(m) = h$.[20]

2. *Second pre-image resistance.* Given message m_1 it is difficult to find a different message m_2 such that $\mathrm{hash}(m_1) = \mathrm{hash}(m_2)$. In other words changing the message leads to changing the hash.

3. *Collision resistance.* It is difficult to find two different messages m_1 and m_2 such that $\mathrm{hash}(m_1) = \mathrm{hash}(m_2)$.

Another desirable property of the hash function is that even small changes in message m are likely to change hash $h = \mathrm{hash}(m)$ significantly. This makes it very unlikely for someone to be able to infer the content of the message from the hash. In summary, the output of hash functions is very much unpredictable (looks random) although it is deterministic. Bitcoin mainly uses SHA-256, a type of Secure Hash Algorithm (SHA-2) designed by the National Security Agency and published by the National Institute of Standards and Technology (see Dang, 2012).

---

[19]The specific class of digital signatures used is called the Elliptical Curve Digital Signature Algorithm. See NSA (2009).

[20]Here and below difficult means statistically unlikely to be achieved through guessing. That is, although random guessing will eventually succeed in finding the proper message, it has such a low probability that the overall likelihood of success in a life-time is statistically negligible.

3.2 A Bitcoin transaction

3.2.1 Bitcoin ownership and Bitcoin addresses

From a technical point of view, bitcoins reside in what is known in the bitcoin system as *bitcoin addresses*. The ownership of a particular amount of bitcoins reduces to the capability of sending payments (over the Bitcoin network) from the bitcoin address(es) with which these bitcoins are being associated. The capability of sending payments from Bitcoin addresses is controlled via digital signatures (we introduced above) that involve pairs of a public key p_k and a private key p_a. In particular, each bitcoin address is indexed by an unique public ID—an alpha numeric identifier which, in fact, corresponds to the public key p_k.[21] The private key p_a, which is the counterpart of p_k, gives control over the bitcoins held in this address. Specifically any payment (message) involving this address as a sending address *has* to be signed with the proper private key to be considered valid. In simple words, owning the bitcoins in a given bitcoin address amounts to knowing the private key which corresponds to the public ID (i.e. the key p_k) of that address.[22]

At any point in time every bitcoin address is associated with a given bitcoin balance which is, in effect, public information. This is the case because any participant in the Bitcoin network can deduce the bitcoin balances following a given transaction history that is recorded in the public ledger. In particular, every existent or proposed (newly broadcast) transaction can be checked for consistency against the preceding history of transactions i.e. it can be verified that the amounts transacted are available in the corresponding bitcoin addresses.

3.2.2 A transaction on the blockchain

Entities engage in transactions on the Bitcoin network through a collection of bitcoin addresses, figuratively called their *wallet*—a set of bitcoin addresses owned by a single entity.[23] In particular, each transaction record involves one or more sending addresses and one or more receiving addresses together with how much each of these addresses send and receive. Figure 3 reflects this description. In the figure, there are two sending

---

[21]An example of such identifier is: `1JArS6jzE3AJ9sZ3aFij1BmTcpFGgN86hA`.

[22]Note that "forgetting" or "losing" the alpha numeric string which represents the private key to a given address implies that the bitcoins associated with this address are *irreversibly* lost.

[23]Here we use "wallet" to refer to the general concept of owning multiple addresses. It is not to be confused by the use of "wallet" or "digital wallet" to refer to computer applications dedicated to managing bitcoin addresses. In reality one can own multiple "digital wallets" from different service providers.

Figure 3: A Bitcoin transaction.

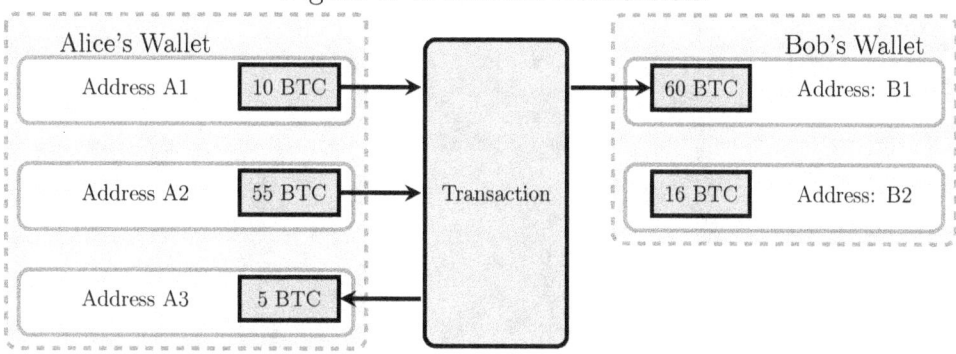

addresses (sending 10 and 55 BTC, respectively) and two receiving addresses (receiving 60 and 5 BTC, respectively). Note that a transaction is the atomic record in the ledger, that is the most detailed level of reporting recorded on the blockchain. An important implication is that because there may be multiple sending and receiving addresses per transaction record, one cannot assign a particular sending address to the funds being sent to a particular receiving address. A further implication of this observation is that one cannot assign serial numbers to bitcoins and trace their paths on the Bitcoin network.

Another important aspect of the way a blockchain is organized is that the boundaries of the wallets are not recorded in the data. Thus, although the ledger is public, one cannot directly observe how bitcoins change ownership. Figure 4 presents a diagram of an actual transaction, that occurred on January 15, 2014. There is one transaction denoted with the white rectangle that involved 14 sending addresses shown in green and 12 receiving addresses shown in blue. In this particular case, one cannot deduce how many entities were involved in the transaction. For example, was there only 1 entity who owned all the sending addresses or were these 14 different entities? We return to this point when we analyze the data from the public ledger.

3.3   The Bitcoin transaction process

The Bitcoin transaction process has mechanisms in place which guarantee that (a) the verification of each transaction is distributed among multiple participants in the network, (b) the recording of each transaction is time discretized, i.e. transactions are linearly ordered with consecutive time stamps, (c) the participants in the payment network compete and are rewarded for recording a transaction, and (d) multiple nodes cross-check

Figure 4: A Bitcoin transaction as seen in the data.

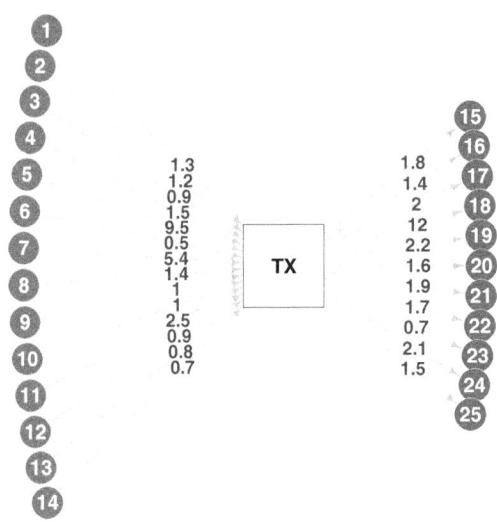

each transaction record.[24] Below we review the Bitcoin transaction process highlighting the above properties.

3.3.1 Initiating a transaction

Suppose that Alice would like to send Bob 1 bitcoin using the Bitcoin network. To do that, both Alice and Bob need to have bitcoin addresses. Call these $\mathtt{address}^{Alice}$ and $\mathtt{address}^{Bob}$. Then Alice needs to issue and (digitally) authenticate a message of the sort

$$\text{``}\mathtt{address}^{Alice}\text{ is sending }\mathtt{address}^{Bob}\text{ 1 bitcoin.''}$$

Because each bitcoin address is identified by a public key, the above message can be represented by figure 5. (recall our discussion from section 3.2.1)

Once Alice signs a transaction message, such as the one in figure 5, with her private key and broadcasts it, every one on the Bitcoin network can verify that it was Alice who issued the message and the message has not been tampered with. Moreover, as we pointed out earlier, the digital signatures ensure that no one else could have signed this message, i.e. Alice cannot deny having signed it.

---

[24]We use node and participants interchangeably. Participants in the payment networks are nodes in the graph induced by the payment activities.

Figure 5: Example of a simple transaction

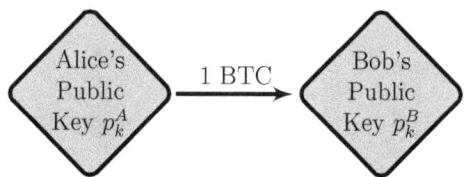

3.3.2 Verifying a transaction

Before executing a transaction (which amounts to recording the transaction on the ledger) the Bitcoin protocol has to verify two aspects of the transaction message: "**address**^{Alice} is sending **address**^{Bob} 1 bitcoin". First, is it Alice who has broadcast the transaction message?[25] As we discussed, the digital signature scheme guarantees that indeed only the owner of the private key for this address could have signed the message. Second, are there enough funds at the sending address to guarantee that the transaction can be completed? Below we discuss how the Bitcoin protocol handles this in a hypothetical scenario, deferring the complexity of the underlying mechanics for a moment.

Suppose there were a single designated participant who maintains all account balances and receives each transaction request. In addition, suppose that the protocol requires that transactions are accepted sequentially, for example, every day there is at most one transaction accepted for verification and clearance. It would have then been trivial in terms of effort for this designated entity to verify the integrity of the transaction request and the availability of funds, and then proceed to record the transaction. Moreover, the fact that transaction requests are accepted sequentially guarantees that duplicated messages and double spending can be readily detected. Note that this hypothetical scenario does not require the books to be either public or private.

More generally, although maintenance of records and verification of transactions are core functions of all electronic payment systems, these functions typically occur through private ledgers maintained by trusted third parties.[26] Decentralized systems such as Bitcoin replace third party intermediaries and the records kept by them with the public ledger maintained by a distributed information system. In particular, the public ledger

---

[25]Note that Bob's authorization is not needed for initiating and eventually recording the transaction.

[26]In payment card systems, for example, banks maintain their own records of the balances of their account-holders. These banks, in turn, use the functionality and record-keeping systems of payment card networks to exchange information needed to allow the transfer of balances between agents (see Prager, Manuszak, Kiser and Borzekowski, 2009).

in the system allows for decentralized approach to transaction message verification.

3.3.3 Blockchain update

After the initial verification of a signed transaction message, a set of participants in the Bitcoin network compete to record the transaction in the blockchain. First, the competing nodes group transactions, which have been broadcast since the last record on the blockchain, in a block of transactions. The block then is used to define a computationally intensive task (to be discussed below). The winner of the competition is the node who *first* solves this task. Once the winner is determined, the transaction record is completed. The winning node is entitled to make the record and collect the reward. It remains to describe the computationally intensive task that defines the competition for recording a block of transactions.

The task on which the nodes compete builds on one of the cryptographic schemes we discussed above—the hash function—and is illustrated in figure 6. First, a block of newly broadcast transactions is used as an input into the cryptographic hash function to obtain a hash called a *digest*. This digest together with a *nounce*—an alpha-numeric string—and the hash of the previous block, are input into another hash function that delivers a blockchain hash of the new block. The task that nodes need to solve comprises finding a nounce such that the blockchain hash of the new block has certain properties (in this case has a certain number of leading zeros).[27] The first competing node to find a desirable nounce broadcasts this information to the rest of the network, and the ledger is updated.[28] This scheme is an implementation of Hashcash, a type of *proof-of-work* system, whose goal is to ensure that computers use a defined number of computational resources to complete some task (see Back, 2002).

The nodes that carry out the proof-of-work process are known in the Bitcoin ecosystem as *miners*. These miners are incentivized to spend computational resources in this process by an award built into the Bitcoin protocol. For the most part the award is a predetermined amount of newly generated bitcoins. The rest of the award, which currently is of much lower value, is voluntary transaction fees that are paid by the initiators

---

[27]Recall the pre-image resistance property from our discussion of cryptographic hashes. Because of this property, the search for nounce amounts to random guessing and is computationally very demanding.

[28]Note that verifying that the proper work was done is very quick because the inputs has to be hashed only once to determine if the output has the correct number of leading zeros. If the information passes this test, then the new block—a group of transactions used to create the digest—is appended to the version of the public ledger held by that node.

Figure 6: Adding a block to the public ledger

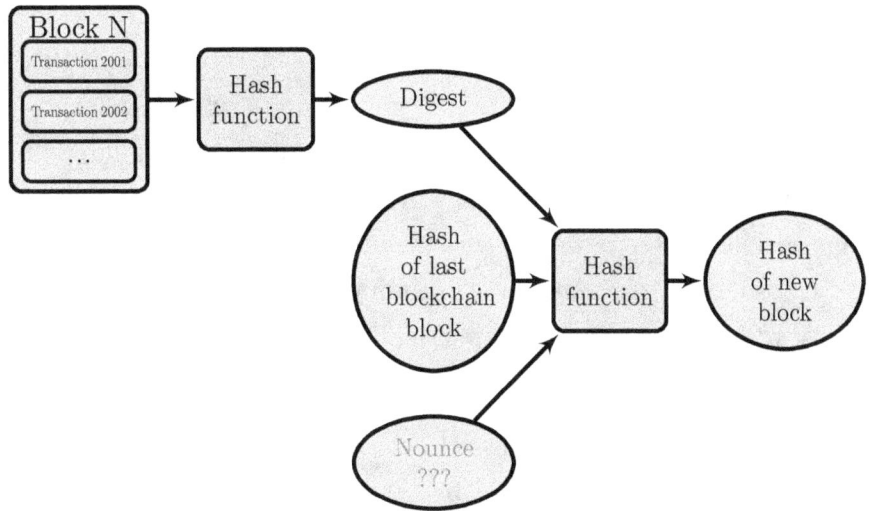

of transactions to the miners in order to process their transactions. The initial idea was that these voluntary fees would replace the coin-generation reward to incentivize miners when that amount goes to zero (Nakamoto, 2009).[29]

4 Data

4.1 Data sources

For our empirical analysis we combine two data sources, the bitcoin ledger and exchange trade data. The public ledger was accessed through the site `blockchain.info`, which provides a human-readable version of the data. These data consist of a complete history of all transactions moving across the Bitcoin network from its inception in 2009 to early-July 2014. We also use transaction-level trade data that have been self-reported by the exchanges and aggregated through the site `bitcoincharts.com`. These data consist of the volume, value, and exchange rate of trades that passed through each of the exchanges. The data starts in mid-2010, with Mt. Gox being one of the earliest exchanges to provide this service, and ends early-July 2014. We analyze data from the six major exchanges: Mt. Gox, Bitstamp, BTCE, BTC China, OKCoin, and Bitfinex.[30]

---

[29]The appendix presents further details on updating the ledger, miners' rewards and development of the bitcoin protocol.

[30]The appendix provides a brief description of each of these exchanges.

4.2 Summary statistics

Table 1 presents summary statistics for the data we analyze. For the blockchain data, we have access to the universe of transactions processed through the Bitcoin payment network. There have been close to 42 million transactions since its inception. The total number of sending addresses is approximately equal to the total number of receiving addresses. The average number of sending addresses per transaction is 1.87, implying that on average senders used more than one sending address per transaction.[31] Also, for an average transaction, the number of sending addresses was below the number of receiving addresses, although there is no particular reason for this.[32]

Looking at the bottom part of table 1, we see that 41 currencies are being traded on 86 exchanges. Comparing the number of transactions recorded on the blockchain and the total number of transactions reported by the exchanges, we see that the majority of transactions on the Bitcoin network occur through exchanges.[33]

5 Empirical analysis

5.1 Daily user estimate

The first question we ask is "How many users operate daily on the Bitcoin network?" As we discussed in section 3.2.2, the public ledger has limited power in addressing this question because it contains the transactions between bitcoin addresses rather than between entities who own the bitcoin addresses. A naive approach would be to treat the number of unique addresses active on a given day (as sending addresses, receiving addresses, or both) as an estimate of the number of users of the system on that day. An alternative approach is to use heuristics to infer common ownership of addresses (see Reid and Harrigan, 2011; Meiklejohn et al., 2013). In particular, we rely on the assumption that if two addresses have *ever* been sending addresses in the *same* transaction, then these are likely

---

[31]Also, the percentage of transactions where there is more than one sending address is 33 percent of the total transactions. See the discussion on consolidating sending addresses below.

[32]There is no particular reason for the number of sending addresses to be above, equal, or below the number of receiving addresses. Recall from the discussion on the structure of transaction records that multiple sending and receiving addresses may be used in a single transaction.

[33]Note that one transaction from the Bitcoin ledger can involve multiple exchanges, which can create double-counting of transactions. This is the most likely explanation of why the total number of reported transactions on the exchanges slightly exceeds the total number of transactions recorded in the ledger. Unfortunately, we cannot estimate the amount of double-counting.

Table 1: Summary statistics

	Statistic	Value
	Transaction Data	
1	Total Transactions	48,214,584
2	Total Number of Sending Addresses	46,551,355
3	Total Number of Receiving Addresses	49,154,169
4	Mean Number of Sending Addresses per Tx	1.91
5	Mean Number of Receiving Addresses per Tx	2.70
	Exchange Data	
6	Number of Exchanges	86
7	Number of Currencies Traded	41
8	Total Transactions	60,362,530
	Trades by Exchange	
9	BitStamp	5,122,767
10	BTCE	16,958,261
11	BTCN	9,074,670
12	MtGox	10,052,536
13	OKCoin	25,402,316
14	Bitfinex	2,398,379
15	Other	9,031,001
	Trades by Currency	
16	USD	34,967,130
17	CNY	34,684,509
18	EUR	3,497,700
19	GBP	607,543
20	Other	4,283,048

to be controlled (owned) by the same entity.[34]

Figure 7 plots the time series of the number of active addresses per day and the number of consolidated ownerships (unique users) using the heuristics above. As we can see, the number of unique users reached close to $100,000$ by the beginning of 2014. Of course this is likely to be an upper bound and it is difficult to judge how tight this upper bound is. However, the more important message of figure 7 is that the number of daily users is likely to have grown *exponentially*, albeit from a low user base, in the past few years.[35] In particular, coarse calculations suggest that the user base has doubled every 8

---

[34]Note that here we focus on daily usage as opposed to those who have ever used Bitcoin.

[35]Of course to conclude that the user base grows exponentially, we need that the ratio active addresses-daily users is either bounded or growing at a polynomial rate, which we believe it is reasonable to assume.

Figure 7: Unique users daily estimate

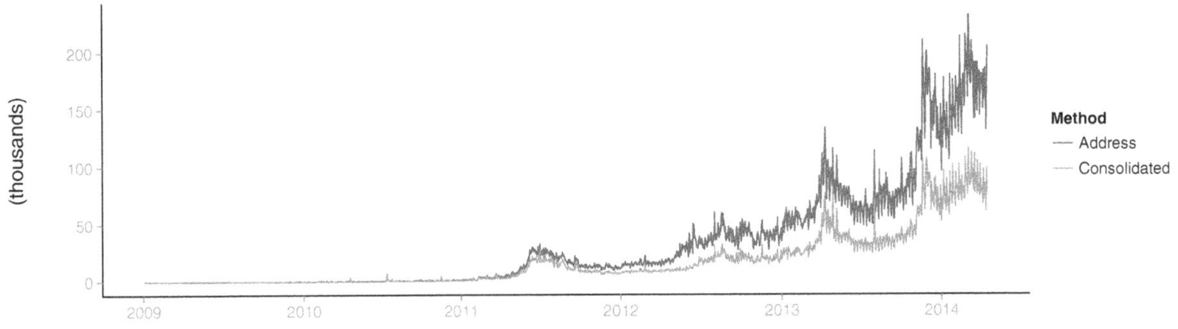

months for the past 3 years.[36]

5.2 Volume and value of daily transactions

Next we look at the metrics of volume, value, and average value shown in figures 8 and 9, which could provide some insight into the amount of activity on the Bitcoin network as well as the use cases. The number of transactions that occurred on a given day peaked at around 80,000 and has remained relatively stable in the past 12–18 months. The volume over the past 12 months totals 21 million and remains negligible compared with the use of alternative payment methods; for example general-purpose cards in the United States alone had a volume of 73.8 billion in 2012 (see Gerdes et al., 2013, page 41). Additionally, the average value of a transaction over the network peaked at almost U.S.$40,000 value equivalent in late 2013. The relatively large average values call for a closer look at the structure of the volume of daily transactions.[37]

5.3 Other measures of usage

As shown in figure 10, transactions across the Bitcoin network were fairly sparse up until mid-2012. For this reason we focus on the period starting with 2012 and examine the

---

[36]It is important to distinguish adoption from daily use. In this respect, we are slightly casual here in that we use the growth of daily use to approximate the growth of the user base (see the previous footnote). On a related note, recall footnote 7 on the presence of network externalities in the bitcoin adoption process.

[37]For comparison, in 2012 the average value of a transaction for general-purpose cards was U.S.$56 (Gerdes et al., 2013, page 41).

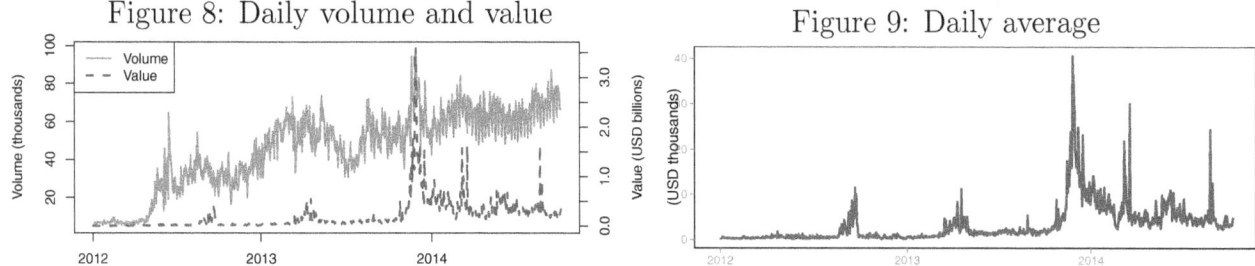

Figure 8: Daily volume and value   Figure 9: Daily average

volume of transactions split out by their value in BTC and USD, figures 11-12. From figure 11 we see that the value distribution of observed transactions in BTC did not vary much in 2013. However, from figure 12, we see substantial variation in the value of transactions in USD, owing to large fluctuations in the exchange rate. This variation is largely the opposite of what we would expect if BTC were a mainstream currency. Somewhat consistent with this observation is that large transfers, i.e. transfers of more than U.S.$100 equivalent value, represent a stable proportion of the activity on the Bitcoin network. While we cannot say what drove this volume of relatively large payments, we conjecture that this part of Bitcoin activity is less likely to involve payments for retail goods and services.

We next examine the pattern of transactions generated by the online gambling service Satoshi Dice and contrast it with the general transaction patterns seen in figures 11 and 12. This is possible in this special case because Satoshi Dice *publicly* advertised the ID (public keys) of its bitcoin addresses.[38] Looking back to figure 10 we see that following an initial period of low activity, where for the most part coins were being generated in the system, there was a sharp increase in the transaction volume in 2012. Specifically, the increase in April 2012 can be attributed to the creation of Satoshi Dice. As figure 13 shows, within weeks of its inception, Satoshi Dice accounted for more than half of all transactions by volume over the network.

To link the volume of Satoshi Dice with the patterns of transactions on figure 12, we note that Satoshi Dice generated exclusively small-value transactions as shown in figure 14. It is reasonable to conclude that almost all small-value transactions on the Bitcoin network before mid-2013 were driven by the online gambling site. Moreover, one cannot readily conclude that this is not still the case. Despite the fact that the volume trailed off after May 2013, when Satoshi Dice stopped accepting U.S. based IP-address requests

---

[38]Satoshi Dice is a gambling service which uniquely takes advantage of the bitcoin protocol to receive payments and reward payouts by publicly posting the public keys of the bitcoin addresses with which it operates.

(see figure 13), the online gambling service may have switched to using non-public Bitcoin addresses with its most loyal users.

Figure 10: Transaction volume

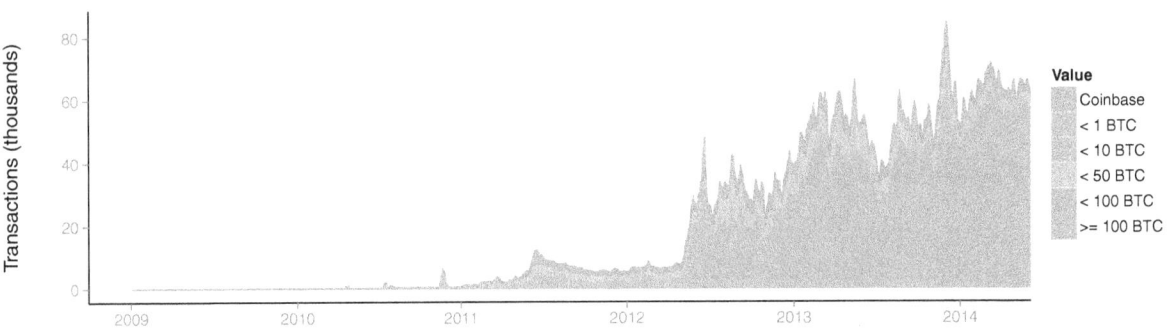

Figure 11: Composition by BTC value   Figure 12: Composition by USD value

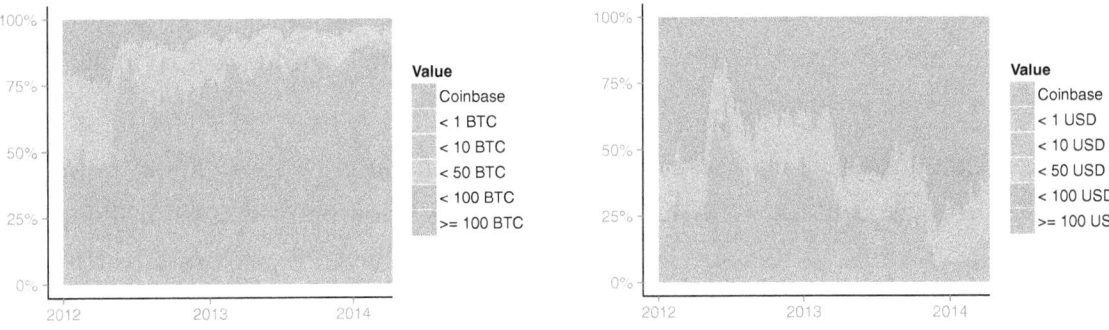

Figure 13: Satoshi Dice vs. Rest   Figure 14: Satoshi Dice volume

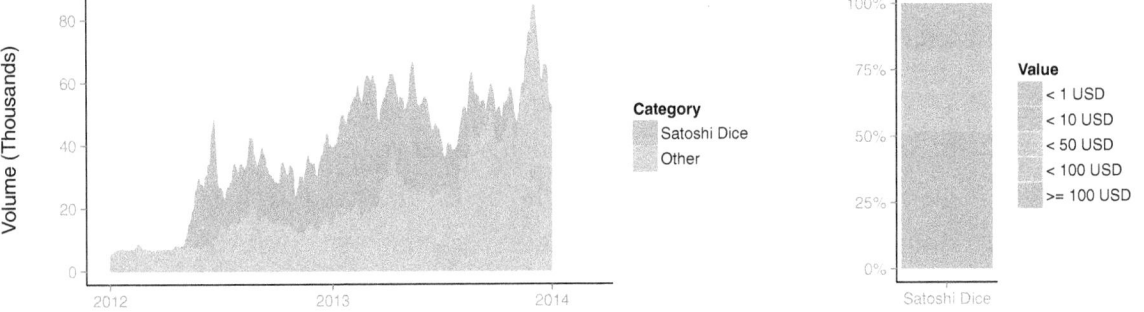

Figure 15: Velocity of addresses

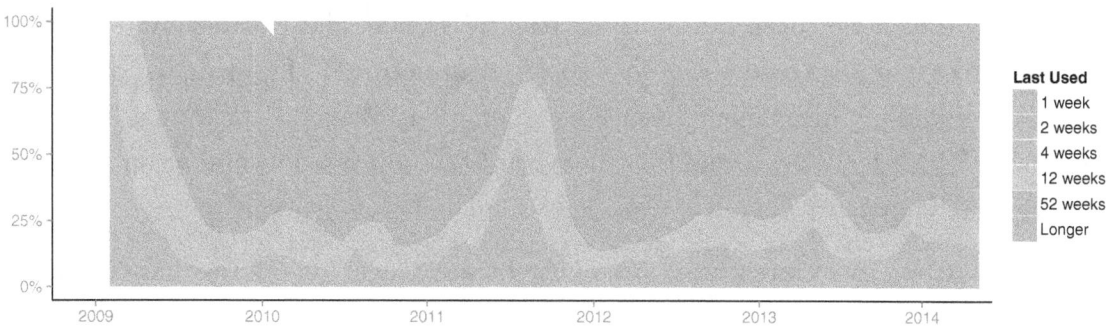

Figure 16: Weighted velocity

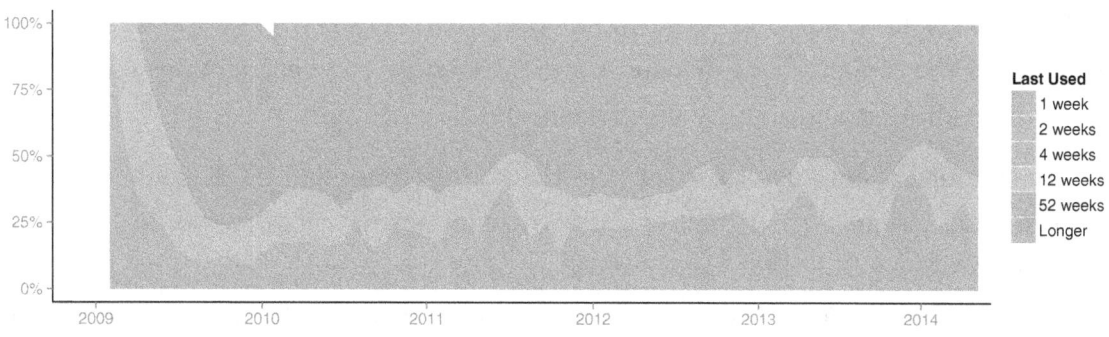

5.4 "Velocity" of bitcoin

We next analyze the patterns of use of Bitcoin addresses. In particular, we are interested in what part of the bitcoin addresses are dormant, i.e. used to store bitcoins without actively transacting. For the addresses that are active, we further investigate their transaction patterns. This analysis will give us an estimate of the extent to which the demand for bitcoins is driven by investment and payment motives. We also provide an estimate of the velocity of bitcoin, i.e. how often bitcoins change addresses. It is important to emphasize that such assessments are possible because of the public availability of transaction data.[39]

Figure 15 examines the degree of activity for the addresses in the network. For each date we partition the volume of addresses with positive balances according to their last

---

[39]Typically, measures of the velocity are obtained *indirectly* through computing, for example, the ratio of quarterly nominal GDP to the quarterly average of M2 money stock (see http://research.stlouisfed.org/fred2/series/M2V).

activity. For example, the addresses that have transacted in the last week are likely to be frequently used (shown with the strip in the bottom). On the other hand, some of the addresses have not been active in the past 52 weeks. Those are likely to serve saving or investment purposes and much less so for transacting.[40] From figure 15 we can see that the volume of "investment" addresses (not used in the last year) has been steadily decreasing. Still, however, around 75 percent of the addresses in operation with positive balances have not been used in a transaction in the last four months.

Figure 16 examines further the size of the balances available in the different addresses: We weight each address by the amount of its bitcoins that day. Note that the addresses that are relatively less active hold disproportionally fewer bitcoins. Specifically, the addresses that transact relatively frequently (at least once in a quarter) hold more than 50 percent of overall bitcoins. On the other hand, a third of the bitcoins are held in addresses that have not transacted in the past year. These overall statistics provide an estimate of the proportion of demand that is driven by payment motives compared with the proportion that is driven by investment motives.[41]

To summarize our analysis so far, less than 50 percent of all bitcoins in circulation are used in transactions. About half of these transactions are small value, i.e. transactions involving less than U.S.$100 value equivalent. For the period for which we have data for Satoshi Dice, almost all of these small value transactions seem to have been related to the online gambling service. Finally, a relatively small number of the large value transactions drive the average transaction value to levels of U.S.$40,000 value equivalent and are not likely to involve retail payments.

5.5 Exchange rates

Exchanges are platforms on which a user who wants to either sell or buy bitcoins with another currency can do so. Much of the media coverage regarding the sky-rocketing price of bitcoin is derived from information coming from these exchanges. As figure 17 shows, the value of bitcoin relative to dollars increased most dramatically in the fourth quarter of 2013. Although trading of the virtual currency began around mid-2010, much of this trading was fairly sparse up until 2013. For this reason we focus on the period starting in January 2013.

---

[40]This includes the value of the so called "lost" bitcoins. Technically, bitcoins in a given address are lost when the private key for that address is lost. Recall the discussion in Section 3.2.1.

[41]Of course, there will always be some ambiguity because holding of balances for transaction purposes is also to some extent an investment.

Figure 17: Exchange rate USD/BTC

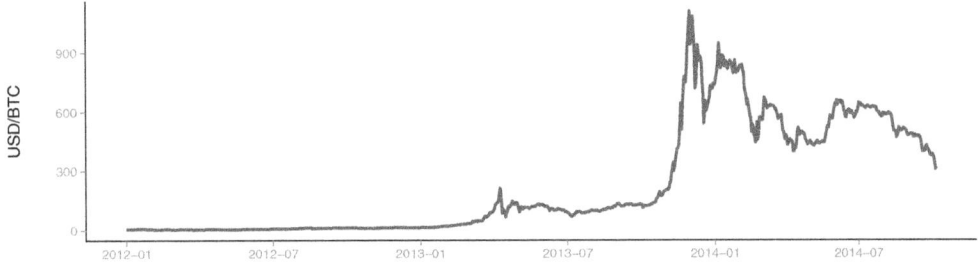

Figure 18: Intra-day volatility USD/BTC

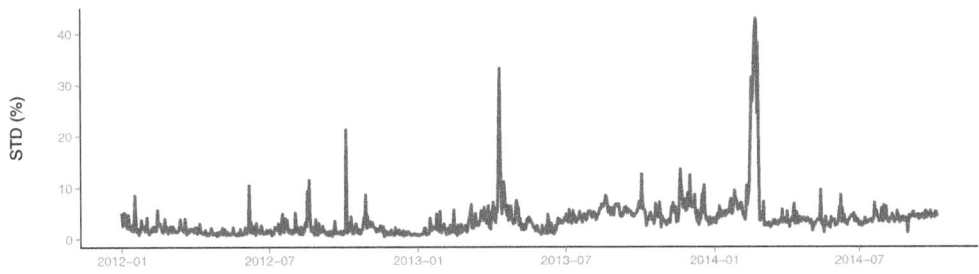

Figure 18 shows the *normalized* daily exchange rate volatility of BTC for USD trades. This measure shows how much the exchange rate fluctuates on a given day as a percentage of the average daily price.[42] Note how remarkably stable this measure of volatility is. With a handful of exceptions, it has stayed below the $12 - 15$ percent limit. It appears that, accounting for the large mean growth of bitcoin value, the risk associated with holding bitcoins for very short periods of time has remained relatively stable.[43] Notably, however, the disruptions in the normalized exchange rate volatility are of substantial magnitude and appear difficult to explain or to predict.

We next ask how "easily" the Bitcoin network can be used to transmit value denom-

---

[42]Hence a standard deviation of 1 percent for a day in which the average price was $100, assuming a normal distribution of exchange rates, would mean that approximately 68.2 percent of trades on that particular day had an implicit exchange rate between $99 and $101 USD per bitcoin.

[43]Recall footnote 9, and note that these findings should not be interpreted to mean that a significant risk does not exist from a variety of factors that may affect the value of bitcoin holdings over short- and medium-term periods. Indeed, little is known about the drivers behind the dynamics of the exchange rate over the first weekend of October 2014 when the exchange rate dropped by almost 20 percent. On the day of the drop the normalized variance was only 16 percent. Finally, we note that assessment of consumers' risks, including the lack of customers' legal protections, is beyond the scope of this work. For a related discussion, see (ICBA, 2014, Virtual Currency: Risk and Regulation) and (EBA, 2014, Opinion on Virtual Currencies).

Figure 19: Exchange rates - converted back to USD

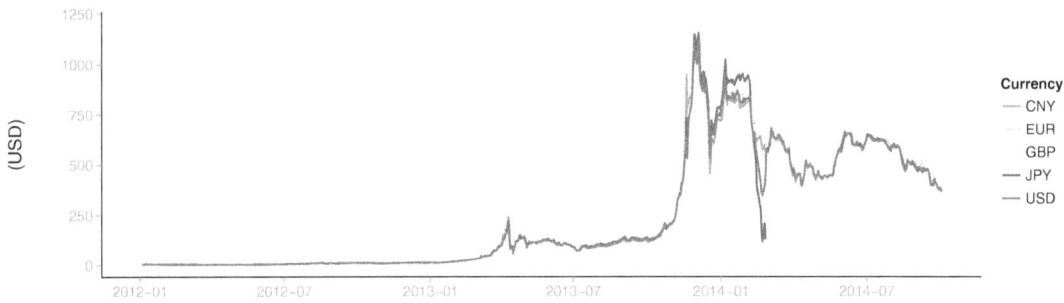

Figure 20: Normalized exchange spread Figure 21: Spread excluding Mt. Gox

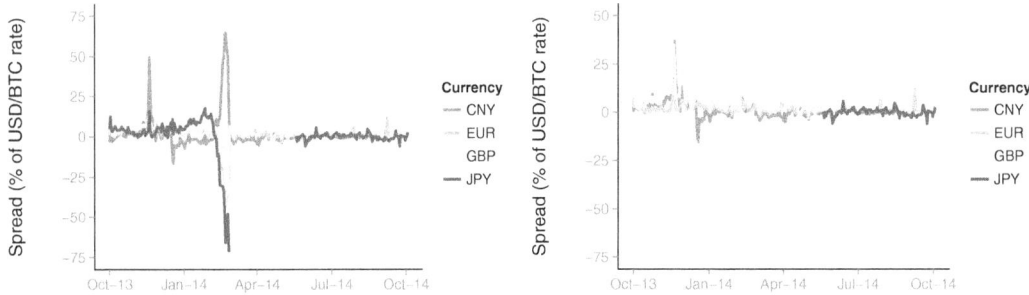

inated in various sovereign currencies, and note that a measure for currency arbitrage (gauging how well bitcoin exchange rates are aligned with those of the cross-exchange rates between major sovereign currencies) may be a good indicator of this. In particular, we note that spreads in highly liquid foreign currency exchange markets are generally very small or else there would be room for arbitrage. Thus, if we were to hypothesize that the bitcoin market is similarly highly liquid, we would expect there to be very little spread between its different exchange rates (more details follow). To examine this hypothesis, we calculate the daily exchange rates in other currencies as a weighted average of the trades that occurred in that currency on a given day. We then take this exchange rate and convert it back to a USD exchange rate with the daily market rate.[44] The results are shown in figures 19-21.

Looking at figure 20, the divergence of the exchange rates starting from the end of 2013 is apparent.[45] One hypothesis to explain this is the collapse of one of the major

---

[44]Exchange rate data used from http://research.stlouisfed.org/fred2/.

[45]We normalize the exchange rates relative to the USD–BTC exchange rate. Additionally, because most of the trading activity occurs starting in the fourth quarter of 2013, we take a closer look at this

exchanges, Mt. Gox, during this period. Even before the bankruptcy filing, it was reported that the troubled exchange stopped allowing withdrawals from its accounts.[46] Because of possible default risk, market participants (including Mt. Gox clients) were trading bitcoins internally at a steep discount out of concern that they might never receive them. To test this hypothesis and correct for this issue, we removed all trades originating from the Mt. Gox exchange in the spread calculation in figure 21. As we can see, the divergence is eliminated and the spread generally decreases. However, we still see a spread that is large relative to other currency markets, at some point reaching above 20 percent. Our initial hypothesis is not supported. We further interpret this evidence as lack of depth of the exchange markets for bitcoins and as costly exchange rather than as unexploited arbitrage opportunities.

5.6 Bitcoin exchanges

The bitcoin exchange market had largely been dominated by Mt. Gox since its inception in 2010, a period that involved relatively little trading activity. This trend changed in 2013 as Mt. Gox lost a large portion of its market share to other exchanges, as shown in figure 22. The change in market share occurred after several highly publicized trading incidents and after legal troubles culminating in the seizure of assets associated with the exchange by U.S. authorities in May 2013 (see Dillet, 2013). The exchange eventually filed for bankruptcy in February 2014 because of the reported loss of 850,000 bitcoins valued at almost 0.5 billion USD at the time (see Hals, 2014). Another large factor reportedly contributing the decline of Mt. Gox was the general increase in trading in other currencies, for example Chinese renminbi (CNY), which were better supported by new exchanges.

As we can see from figure 23, the U.S. dollar was the dominant exchange currency used in trading for a majority of the period before the fourth quarter of 2013. At that time there was a large influx of trading activity involving the CNY. It is important to note that trade in a specific currency does not necessarily mean the transaction originated in the country that issues the currency, because some traders may opt to use a more common currency over their local currency. The initial spike of trading of CNY toward the end of 2013 was followed by a rapid decrease in activity, likely due to Chinese authorities cracking down on digital currencies by banning financial intermediaries from dealing with exchanges (see The Economist, 2014). Since then, trading in CNY has resumed pace,

---

period in figure 20.

[46]See https://en.bitcoin.it/wiki/MtGox.

Figure 22: Weekly trading value by exchange

Figure 23: Weekly trading value by currency

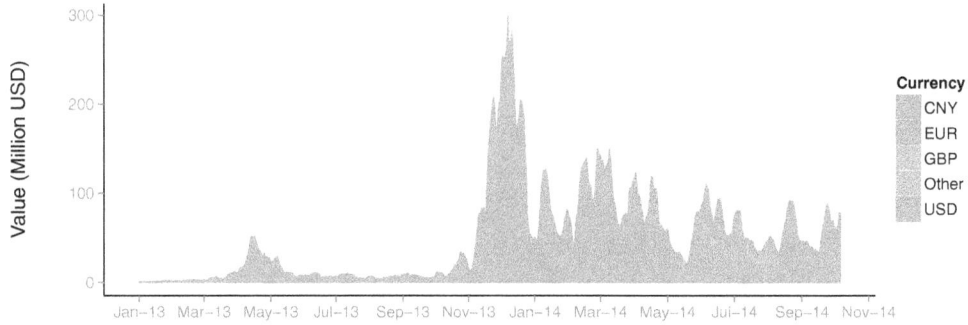

overtaking the USD as the the main trading currency for much of 2014.[47]

6   Concluding remarks

Motivated by recent developments in the Bitcoin ecosystem, this paper provides the necessary technical background to understand basic Bitcoin operations and documents a set of empirical regularities related to Bitcoin usage. Our empirical analysis relies on publicly available data from the Bitcoin system, and is intended to stimulate substantive economic research.

Broadly speaking, our empirical exercise documents general patterns of Bitcoin usage, and examines the use of Bitcoin for investment and payment purposes. We find that while

---

[47]For more on bitcoin exchanges see BTCwiki (2014b) and BTC-Planet (2014)

the number of daily users may have doubled every eight months, the transaction volume is negligible compared to the domestic volume of U.S. payment systems. Our analysis of data from the Bitcoin system further suggests that Bitcoin is still barely used for payments for goods and services. In addition, the patterns of circulations of bitcions and the dynamics of the bitcoin exchange rate are consistent with low usage of Bitcoin for retail payment transactions. Finally, we provide evidence that the exchange rates between bitcoin and other currencies are not well aligned, which we interpret as a lack of depth of the exchange markets and as costly exchange rather than unexploited arbitrage opportunities.

A Events in the Bitcoin timeline

- January 2009: Bitcoin protocol is released and the first coins are generated by miners.

- July 2010: Mt. Gox launches an exchange to trade bitcoins.

- February 2011: Silk Road, an online marketplace mainly for illegal activities, is founded.

- June 2011: BTC China exchange is founded.

- July 2011: BTCE, a Bulgarian-based cryptocurrency exchange, is launched.

- August 2011: Bitstamp is founded in Slovenia and in April 2013 is moved to the U.K.

- October 2011: Litecoin is released as a modified version of the original Bitcoin code by a former Google employee.

- April 2012: Satoshi Dice, the most popular bitcoin online gambling service, begins operations.

- February 2013: New anti-money laundering laws causes Dwolla to cancel transactions from Mt. Gox.

- April 2013: Mt. Gox suspends trading for a day causing the price of the currency to drop sharply.

- March 2013: FinCEN defines its position on virtual currency and outlines regulatory response.

- May 2013: Satoshi Dice blocks all incoming U.S. based IP address traffic citing possible legal concerns

- September 2013: Federal Reserve Chairman Bernanke sends a letter to Congress on virtual currency.

- October 2013: The FBI shuts down Silk Road, seizing 26,000 BTC worth approximately $3.6 million USD at the time.

- December 2013: Chinese authorities prohibit banks and payment institutions in the country from dealing in bitcoins.

- February 2014: Mt. Gox files for bankruptcy after disclosing the loss of 850,000 BTC valued at almost U.S.$500 million at the time.

- February 2014: Bitstamp (the largest exchange at this time by the value of processed transactions) suspends withdrawals for several days after facing a distributed DOS attack.

- March 2014: IRS issues guidance on virtual currencies.

- June 2014: Mining pool temporarily reaches 51% network computing power.

- July 2014: New York regulators propose new rules to govern virtual currency businesses.

B Further details on maintaining the ledger

B.1 Blockchain updating

In this section we examine the process for reaching a consensus on the ledger. The main rule for determining the legitimate ledger is that it is the one that took the most cumulative work to generate. Work is a function of the difficulty in finding a satisfactory nounce, which produces a hash with desirable properties. This difficulty changes dynamically to average 10-minute validation of blocks. Because work in the form of computational power is expended to encode a block, this work is added to the overall work of the blockchain that it is a part of. The incremental difficulty of a block is a (monotone) function of the number of leading zeros in its nounce (recall figure 6). The cumulative difficulty is given by the sum of the incremental difficulty of all the blocks in a chain (BTCwiki, 2014a). Moving forward, we will use d to generically denote each block's incremental difficulty.

Figure 24: Blockchain Updating

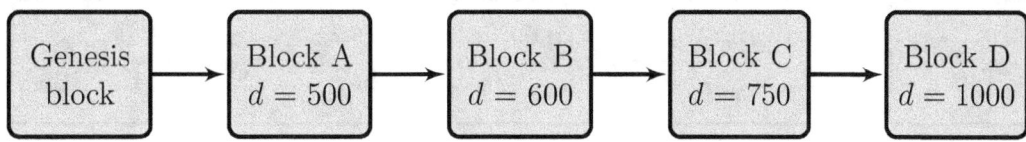

To demonstrate the process of coming to a consensus on the correct ledger, consider adding a new block to the ledger on figure 24. Assume that block A is the current block and the miners are competing to add to this block. In the usual case a miner "wins" and broadcasts a new block B to the network, which is subsequently incorporated into the chain and adds to its difficulty. To verify a given version of the ledger, one needs to confirm that the given ledger has the highest cumulative difficulty. Thus, an attacker who seeks to manipulate the ledger has to propose one with higher difficulty than the main ledger. This would only be possible if the attacker had more computational power than (all) the other nodes in the network.

Blockchain forking

Let us consider the special case where two miners encode two different blocks and broadcast them nearly simultaneously, and assume that both blocks are with the same difficulty. This situation is depicted in figure 25 where the last block before the forking is B. The forking results in parts of the network adding block C.1 to their ledger and some adding block C.2 to their ledger. To resolve this issue, since a common ledger is the goal, the process waits for the following block to be added to either block C.1 or C.2 with two different parts of the network working on each. Suppose that the miners who are working on block C.2 successfully encode a new block D before the miners working on block C.1. In this case the network will accept the chain with the blocks A, B, C.2, D as the main ledger because it has the highest difficulty and will mark block C.1 as an orphan block. As the time passes more blocks "seal" a given transaction on the blockchain so that there is more certainty that this transaction will remain encoded in the main ledger.

Figure 25: Blockchain forking

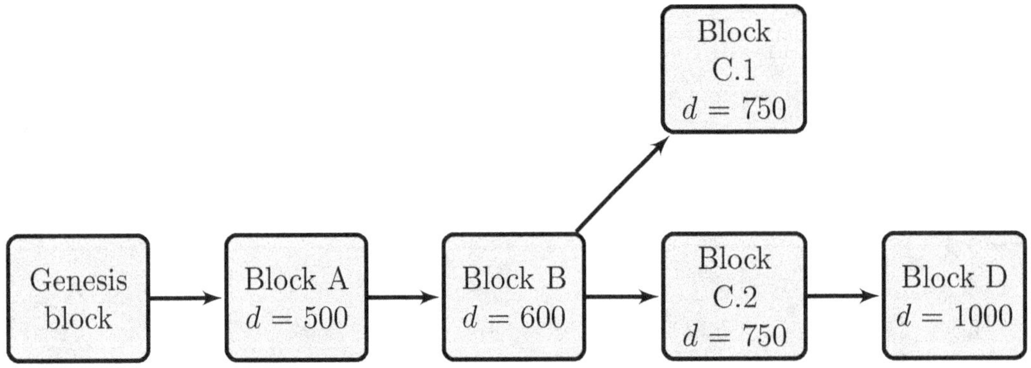

Note that this way of determining the correct ledger makes the protocol secure against certain types of attacks. For instance an attacker who has the desire to modify previous blocks in the blockchain would need to re-encode the targeted blocks along with all subsequent blocks thus, in essence, proposing a new blockchain. Importantly, the cumulative difficulty of this modified blockchain has to surpasses that of the main ledger, which is nearly (statistically) impossible. However, if the attacker controls at least 51 percent of the computing power on the network, it is possible for the attacker to outpace the rest of the miners in the network and to encode a separate block with higher difficulty than the main block. Even in this situation the attacker cannot arbitrarily transfer value between addresses because private keys are still needed to sign transactions. Instead the attacker can prevent currently-broadcast transactions from being recorded in the blockchain or exclude past (already recorded) transactions from the blockchain.[48]

B.2   Miner incentives and bitcoin supply

The bitcoin miners who carry out the proof-of-work algorithm are essential for the Bitcoin scheme, which incorporates (currently substantial) economic rewards for miners participation. Miners' rewards come in two forms: transaction fees and bitcoin generation. The magnitude of the transaction fees per block of transactions has remained stable and relatively low (figure 26). In contrast, from the end of 2013 the USD value equivalent of the newly minted bitoins rewarded per block grew substantially and, currently, is close to U.S.$10,000 equivalent value per block (figure 27).[49] This number is very close to what ultimately is collected by miners who currently make a block-record every 10 minutes. These rates imply a total reward of U.S.$1,440,000 equivalent value per day and an average reward of U.S.$25 equivalent value per transaction (see figure 28). These relatively large rewards, and the associated electricity and hardware costs for executing the proof-of-work computations, have raised concerns about the efficiency of the Bitcoin scheme (see Levine, 2014).[50]

Historically, transaction fees were designed to take the place of newly minted bitcoins in the miners' rewards because of the commitment of the Bitcoin scheme to reducing the newly minted bitcoins to zero (Nakamoto, 2009). The transaction fees are voluntarily allocated by the sender of a transaction and, currently, are about 0.5 percent of the overall reward (see figure 29). Thus, there will need to be a significant increase in the fee per

---

[48]The latter is equivalent to implicitly reversing a transaction.

[49]This is due to the large appreciation in the BTC-USD exchange rate. The amount of newly minted bitcoins per block of transactions remained the same for this period.

[50]Note that large miners' rewards do not directly translate to large costs for the Bitcoin users because miners' rewards are financed almost exclusively by newly minted bitcoins. However, large miners' rewards stimulate the competition between miners, who need to incur higher electricity and hardware costs in order to maintain their competitiveness for doing the proof-of-work computations.

Figure 26: Fee per block (USD value equivalent)

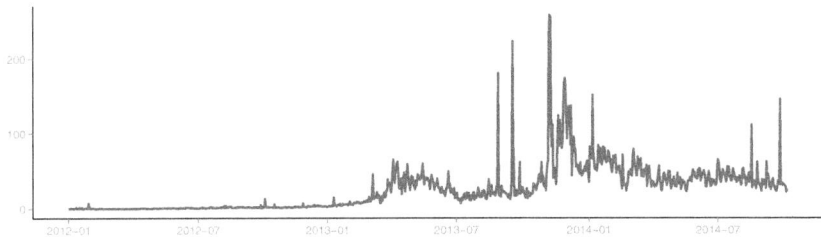

Figure 27: Newly minted bitcoins per block (USD value equivalent)

Figure 28: Total miners' rewards per transaction (USD value equivalent)

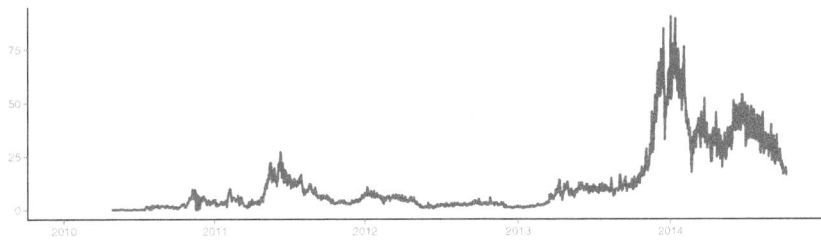

Figure 29: Ratio fee/new BTC per block

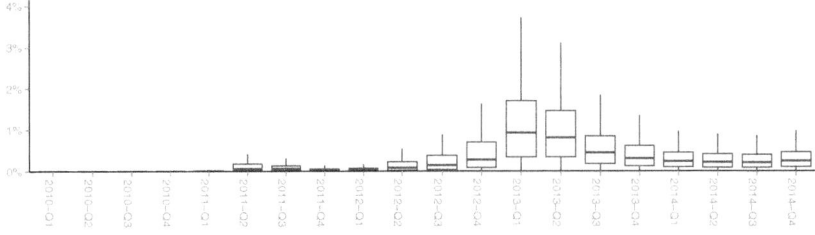

Note to figures 26, 27, and 28. *Calculations for miner reward in USD value equivalent are not available before mid-2010 because of the lack of exchange rate data.*

Figure 30: BTC in circulation

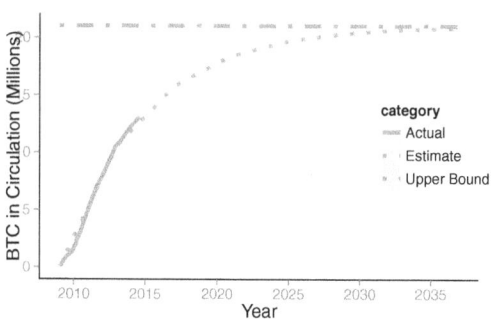 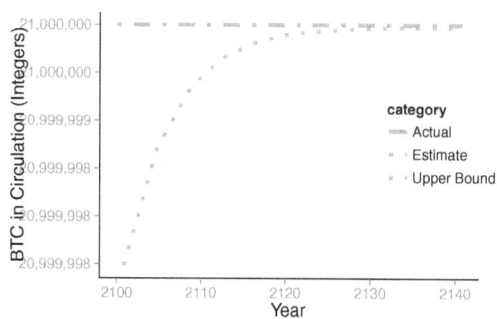

Note: *The left graph presents the actual and the targeted amounts of bitcoins in circulation. The right graph zooms in the period from 2100 to 2140. Note that the projected growth of the bitcoin supply for the last 40 years is only 2 bitcoins.*

transaction or in the volume of transactions in order to maintain the current level of compensation for miners.

As we noted in the overview section, the procedure for rewarding those who make records on the blockchain appears to "hard-code" the growth of the bitcoin supply. In particular, because the rate of making transaction records is committed to a given level, there is some certainty about the rate of growth of bitcoins and the amount of bitcoins in circulation. Figure 30 plots the past dynamics of the bitcoins in circulation together with the declared rule of growth, whereby every four years the rate of minting new bitcoins decreases by half.[51] The figure suggests that the upper bound of 21 million BTC in circulation will be reached in 2140. We note in passing that on the right graph of figure 30, which zooms in the period from 2100 to 2140, the projected growth of the bitcoin supply for the last 40 years is only 2 bitcoins.[52]

B.3   Development of the protocol

We can think of the bitcoin protocol as a set of rules upon which parties agree. As with all other systems of rules, the bitcoin protocol was not built perfectly from the start and thus needs updating to adapt to a dynamic, real-world environment. The updating uses an open source model similar to the ones used for the ongoing development of Linux, an

---

[51]See https://bitcoin.org/en/faq.

[52]Data for the targeted amount of bitcoins is taken from https://en.bitcoin.it/wiki/Controlled_supply.

Figure 31: Updates to source code by contributors

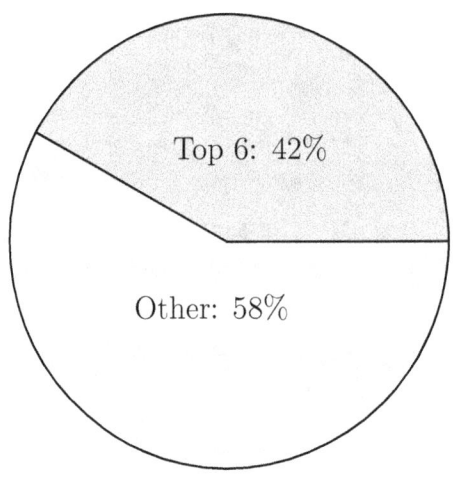

open source operating system. The process mirrors the consensus-building deployed in the bitcoin protocol itself to come to an agreement on valid transactions.

We will illustrate this process through the example in figure 32. Assume that everyone starts off with the same set of rules or version of the protocol. There can theoretically be many forums in which new rules are debated, however, in practice it makes more sense to have these debates in one place. This chosen forum would be controlled by moderators who are trusted voices in the Bitcoin community. To start the process, an addition or change in the current rules of the protocol is proposed and discussed in the forum. The change is then added to the next version release or left out, depending on the reaction of the community, but ultimately at the choice of the moderator. The release then goes through a final process of adoption in which parties implicitly "vote" by either adopting the changes in the release or rejecting them. Stepping back, we can see that all the rules outlined in the protocol are malleable if a majority of the parties involved come to a consensus. Researchers have pointed out that in this sense, the protocol will eventually develop necessary governance structures for the continuity of the system (Kroll, Davey and Felton, 2013).

In the actual implementation, the bitcoin source code is stored in an online repository (GitHub) that is controlled by the members of what we will refer to as the core development team. We can consider this to be the current main branch of rules that a majority of the parties agree to abide by, as well as the central forum in which proposals for changes are made. As we can see from figure 31, this core group is responsible for a large number of the proposed changes to the protocol since its initial release. While

Figure 32: Protocol development

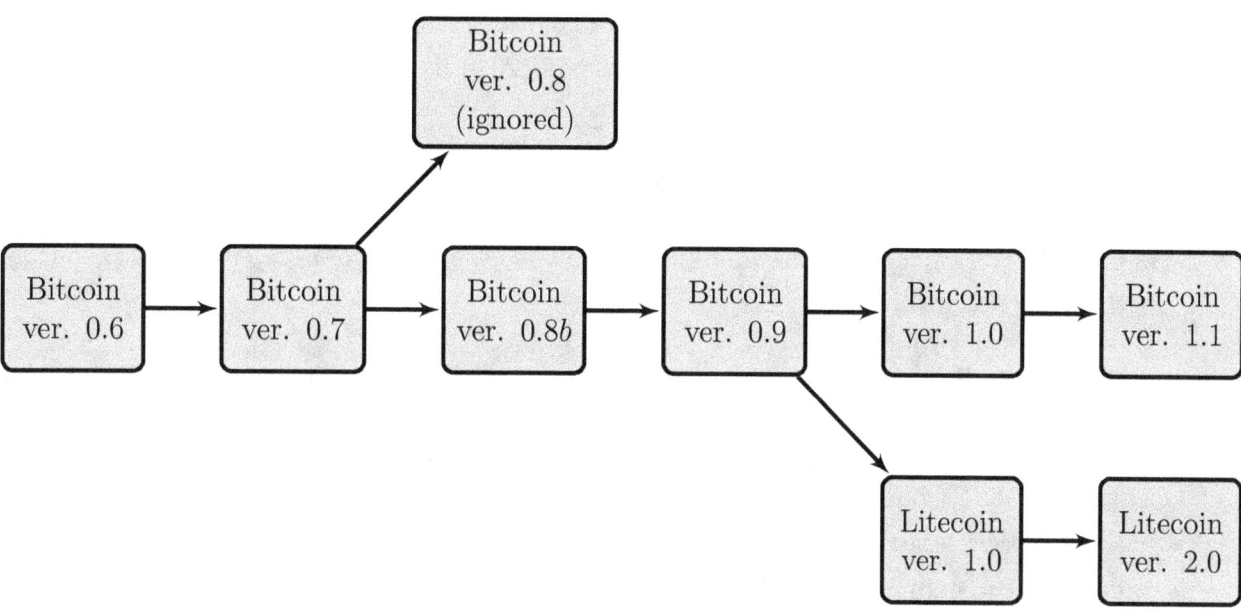

ownership of the repository falls in the hands of one or a few people, it is important to note that adoption of changes requires a consensus from the community. For instance, figure 32 shows a hypothetical example in which if version 0.8 of bitcoin was released with questionable changes, the people in the network can choose to reject the version and continue running version 0.7 or create another, separate version 0.8b to adopt without needing the approval of the core development team. Kroll et al. (2013) use the emergence of this group, composed of well respected developers in the bitcoin community, as an early form of governance for the protocol.

References

Back, Adam, "Hashcash-a denial of service counter-measure," 2002. Available at `http://www.hashcash.org/papers/hashcash.pdf` (2014-09-17).

BTC-Planet, "Complete List of Bitcoin Exchanges," Available at `http://planetbtc.com/complete-list-of-bitcoin-exchanges/` (2014-09-17) 2014.

BTCwiki, "Difficulty," Available at `https://en.bitcoin.it/wiki/Difficulty` (2014/04/15) 2014.

_ , "Exchanges," Available at `https://en.bitcoin.it/wiki/Category:Exchanges` (2014-09-17) 2014.

CoinDesk, "CoinDesk State of Bitcoin Q2 2014," Technical Report, CoinDesk July 2014. Available at `http://www.coindesk.com/state-of-bitcoin-q2-2014-report-expanding-bitcoin-economy/` (2014-09-17).

Dang, Quynh, "Recommendation for Applications Using Approved Hash Algorithms," Technical Report, National Institute of Standards and Technology August 2012.

Dillet, Romain, "Feds Seize Assets From Mt. Goxs Dwolla Account, Accuse It Of Violating Money Transfer Regulations," *TechCrunch*, May 2013. Available at http://techcrunch.com/2013/05/16/mt-gox-dwolla-account-money-seizure/ (2014-04-17).

EBA, "EBA Opinion on Virtual Currencies," Technical Report, European Banking Authority July 2014. Available at `http://www.eba.europa.eu/documents/10180/657547/EBA-Op-2014-08+Opinion+on+Virtual+Currencies.pdf` (2014-09-17).

ECB, "Virtual Currency Schemes," Technical Report, European Central Bank October 2012. Available at `www.ecb.europa.eu/pub/pdf/other/virtualcurrencyschemes201210en.pdf` (2014-09-17).

GAO, "Virtual Currencies: Emerging Regulatory, Law Enforcement, and Consumer Protection Challenges," Technical Report, United States Government Accountability Office May 2014. Available at `www.gao.gov/assets/670/663678.pdf` (2014-09-17).

Gerdes, Geoffrey R., May X. Liu, Jason P. Berkenpas, Matthew C. Chen Matthew C. Hayward, James M. McKee, Scott Drake, Patrick Dyer, Dave Brangaccio, and Nancy Donahue, "Recent and Long-Term Payment Trends in the

Unitred States: 2003-2012," Technical Report, Federal Reserve System December 2013. Available at `http://www.frbservices.org/files/communications/pdf/research/2013_payments_study_summary.pdf` (2014-09-17).

Hals, Tom, "Mt. Gox files U.S. bankruptcy, opponents call it a ruse," *Reuters*, March 2014. Available at `http://www.reuters.com/article/2014/03/10/us-bitcoin-mtgox-bankruptcy-idUSBREA290WU20140310` (2014-04-17).

ICBA, "Virtual Currency: Risk and Regulation," Technical Report, The Clearing House June 2014. Available at `www.theclearinghouse.org/~/media/Files/Research/20140623%20Virtual%20Currency%20White%20Paper.pdf` (2014-09-17).

Karame, Ghassan O., Elli Androulaki, and Srdjan Capkun, "Two Bitcoins at the Price of One? Double-Spending Attacks on Fast Payments in Bitcoin," 2012. Available at `http://eprint.iacr.org/2012/248.pdf` (2014-09-17).

Kroll, Joshua A., Ian C. Davey, and Edward W. Felton, "The Economics of Bitcoin Mining, or Bitcoin in the Presence of Adversaries," *Proceedings of WEIS. Vol. 2013*, 2013.

Levine, Matt, "Bitcoin Is an Expensive Way to Pay for Stuff," *BloombergView*, 2014. Available at `http://www.bloombergview.com/articles/2014-01-02/bitcoin-is-an-expensive-way-to-pay-for-stuff` (2014-09-17).

Lo, Stepahanie and J. Christina Wang, "Bitcoin as Money?," *Federal Reserve Bank of Boston, Current Pllicy Perspectives No 14-4*, 2014, *14*.

Meiklejohn, Sarah, Marjori Pomarole, Grant Jordan, Kirill Levchenko, Damon McCoyy, Geoffrey M. Voelker, and Stefan Savage, "A fistful of bitcoins: characterizing payments among men with no names," *Proceedings of the 2013 conference on Internet measurement conference*, 2013.

Nakamoto, Satoshi, "Bitcoin: A Peer-to-Peer Electronic Cash System," 2009. Unpublished Manuscript.

NSA, "The Case for Elliptical Curve Crytography," Technical Report, National Security Agency January 2009.

Prager, Robin A., Mark D. Manuszak, Elizabeth K. Kiser, and Ron Borzekowski, "Interchange Fees and Payment Card Networks: Economics, Industry

Developments, and Policy Issues," *Finance and Economics Discussion Series, Board of Governors of the Federal Reserve System (U.S.).*, 2009, *23*.

Reid, Fergal and Martin Harrigan, "An Analysis of Anonymity in the Bitcoin System," *CoRR*, 2011, *abs/1107.4524*.

The Economist, "A dream dispelled : Chinese regulators make life hard for crypto-currencies," *The Economist*, April 2014. Available at http://www.economist.com/news/finance-and-economics/21600736-chinese-regulators-make-life-hard-crypto-currencies-dream-dispelled (2014-04-17).

Yermack, David, "Is Bitcoin a Real Currency? An economic appraisal," *NBER working paper*, December 2013.